AF271324

PERSONAL INFORMATION

Name:

Address:

Telephone: Email:

Employer:

Address:

Telephone: Email:

MEDICAL INFORMATION

Physician: Telephone:

Allergies:

Medications:

Blood Type:

Insurer:

IN CASE OF EMERGENCY, NOTIFY

Name:

Address:

Telephone: Relationship:

ISBN 978-1-63609-581-3

Published by Barbour Publishing, Inc., 1810 Barbour Drive, Uhrichsville, Ohio 44683, www.barbourbooks.com

Our mission is to inspire the world with the life-changing message of the Bible.

Printed in China.

PEACE, BE STILL

"Be still, and know that I am God."
Psalm 46:10 esv

Some days peace feels as elusive as a bird taking flight. You'd like to grab hold of it, to hang on for dear life, but with so many distractions tugging at you, is such a thing even possible?

Absolutely! God created you to live in peace despite the craziness, the busyness, the hectic lifestyle, the family commitments, the work overload. In the middle of the chaos, in the very center of the storm, as you face Goliath-sized problems, you can find true and lasting peace in your Savior's arms.

God's call to peace requires one very special thing of you—that you draw near to Him. There, in that quiet place, He will give you the tools you need to release the tension and replace it with His supernatural peace.

Are you ready to be transformed? Allow this planner to guide you, as you enter into the heavenly Father's presence. May every day of 2024 be overflowing with a God-breathed peace that passes all understanding!

YEAR AT A GLANCE

JANUARY

S	M	T	W	T	F	S
	1	2	3	4	5	6
7	8	9	10	11	12	13
14	15	16	17	18	19	20
21	22	23	24	25	26	27
28	29	30	31			

FEBRUARY

S	M	T	W	T	F	S
				1	2	3
4	5	6	7	8	9	10
11	12	13	14	15	16	17
18	19	20	21	22	23	24
25	26	27	28	29		

MAY

S	M	T	W	T	F	S
			1	2	3	4
5	6	7	8	9	10	11
12	13	14	15	16	17	18
19	20	21	22	23	24	25
26	27	28	29	30	31	

JUNE

S	M	T	W	T	F	S
						1
2	3	4	5	6	7	8
9	10	11	12	13	14	15
16	17	18	19	20	21	22
23	24	25	26	27	28	29
30						

SEPTEMBER

S	M	T	W	T	F	S
1	2	3	4	5	6	7
8	9	10	11	12	13	14
15	16	17	18	19	20	21
22	23	24	25	26	27	28
29	30					

OCTOBER

S	M	T	W	T	F	S
		1	2	3	4	5
6	7	8	9	10	11	12
13	14	15	16	17	18	19
20	21	22	23	24	25	26
27	28	29	30	31		

2024

MARCH

S	M	T	W	T	F	S
					1	2
3	4	5	6	7	8	9
10	11	12	13	14	15	16
17	18	19	20	21	22	23
24	25	26	27	28	29	30
31						

APRIL

S	M	T	W	T	F	S
	1	2	3	4	5	6
7	8	9	10	11	12	13
14	15	16	17	18	19	20
21	22	23	24	25	26	27
28	29	30				

JULY

S	M	T	W	T	F	S
	1	2	3	4	5	6
7	8	9	10	11	12	13
14	15	16	17	18	19	20
21	22	23	24	25	26	27
28	29	30	31			

AUGUST

S	M	T	W	T	F	S
				1	2	3
4	5	6	7	8	9	10
11	12	13	14	15	16	17
18	19	20	21	22	23	24
25	26	27	28	29	30	31

NOVEMBER

S	M	T	W	T	F	S
					1	2
3	4	5	6	7	8	9
10	11	12	13	14	15	16
17	18	19	20	21	22	23
24	25	26	27	28	29	30

DECEMBER

S	M	T	W	T	F	S
1	2	3	4	5	6	7
8	9	10	11	12	13	14
15	16	17	18	19	20	21
22	23	24	25	26	27	28
29	30	31				

AUGUST 2023

SUNDAY	MONDAY	TUESDAY	WEDNESDAY
30	31	1	2
6	7	8	9
13	14	15	16
20	21	22	23
27	28	29	30

THURSDAY	FRIDAY	SATURDAY
3	4	5
10	11	12
17	18	19
24	25	26
31	1	2

JULY

S	M	T	W	T	F	S
						1
2	3	4	5	6	7	8
9	10	11	12	13	14	15
16	17	18	19	20	21	22
23	24	25	26	27	28	29
30	31					

SEPTEMBER

S	M	T	W	T	F	S
					1	2
3	4	5	6	7	8	9
10	11	12	13	14	15	16
17	18	19	20	21	22	23
24	25	26	27	28	29	30

BLESSED ASSURANCE!

Blessed assurance! That's what I have in You, Lord. I can place my trust in no other. (Boy, have I tried and failed! The stories I could tell!)

Now that I've tasted and seen Your goodness, Your grace, Your mercy, I can set my heart on none but You. When I'm faithful to do that, You give me assurance of Your presence, Your caring, and Your great love. It's so easy to trust the one who loves me so abundantly!

Walking in the assurance of Your great love also means that I can walk in peace from day to day. I don't have to wonder if You're going to give up on me. I know You won't! I can know for sure that You will never leave me or forsake me, that You are my constant companion, the lover of my soul.

How I worship You today and all days, precious Lord! I once again commit to place my trust solely in You.

Amen.

GOALS for this MONTH

- [ ] ....
- [ ] ....
- [ ] ....
- [ ] ....
- [ ] ....
- [ ] ....
- [ ] ....
- [ ] ....
- [ ] ....
- [ ] ....
- [ ] ....
- [ ] ....
- [ ] ....
- [ ] ....

Trust in the LORD with all your heart,
and do not lean on your own understanding.

PROVERBS 3:5 ESV

Heavenly Father, in the name of Jesus, giants
are defeated. Mountains move. They crumble
with just the whisper of Your name, Lord!

SUNDAY, July 30

MONDAY, July 31

TUESDAY, August 1

WEDNESDAY, August 2

THURSDAY, August 3

FRIDAY, August 4

SATURDAY, August 5

Some trust in chariots and some in horses,
but we trust in the name of the LORD our God.
PSALM 20:7 ESV

Father, You lead me down a fragrant path
toward meadows where I can rest and recline
in Your presence. Your path brings peace,
so I choose to follow hard after You.

SUNDAY, August 6

....
....
....
....

MONDAY, August 7

....
....
....
....

TUESDAY, August 8

....
....
....
....

WEDNESDAY, August 9

THURSDAY, August 10

FRIDAY, August 11

SATURDAY, August 12

*Be watchful, stand firm in
the faith. . .be strong.*
1 Corinthians 16:13 esv

Lord, You are my great Redeemer.
My forgiver. My hope. You're the one who
can bring peace when no one else can.

SUNDAY, August 13

....
....
....
....

MONDAY, August 14

....
....
....
....

TUESDAY, August 15

....
....
....
....

WEDNESDAY, August 16

THURSDAY, August 17

FRIDAY, August 18

SATURDAY, August 19

How great is the goodness you have stored up for those who fear you. You lavish it on those who come to you for protection, blessing them before the watching world.
PSALM 31:19 NLT

When I think of all You're capable of, Father, when I'm reminded of all You've done, it reminds me that You are capable of re-creating me. You can take the messes I've made and breathe new life into them.

SUNDAY, August 20

....

....

....

....

MONDAY, August 21

....

....

....

....

TUESDAY, August 22

....

....

....

....

WEDNESDAY, August 23

THURSDAY, August 24

FRIDAY, August 25

SATURDAY, August 26

I praise you, for I am fearfully and wonderfully made. Wonderful are your works; my soul knows it very well.
PSALM 139:14 ESV

My life is in Your hands, Lord, not mine. I try to maneuver, to make things happen, but nothing I do compares to what You do. With just a word, You can change everything. You *have* changed everything.

SUNDAY, August 27

....

....

....

....

MONDAY, August 28

....

....

....

....

TUESDAY, August 29

....

....

....

....

WEDNESDAY, August 30

THURSDAY, August 31

FRIDAY, September 1

SATURDAY, September 2

*Let us keep looking to Jesus. Our faith comes
from Him and He is the One Who makes it
perfect. He did not give up when He had to
suffer shame and die on a cross. He knew
of the joy that would be His later. Now
He is sitting at the right side of God.*
HEBREWS 12:2 NLV

SEPTEMBER 2023

SUNDAY	MONDAY	TUESDAY	WEDNESDAY
27	28	29	30
3	4 *Labor Day*	5	6
10	11	12	13
17	18	19	20
24	25	26	27

THURSDAY	FRIDAY	SATURDAY
31	1	2
7	8	9
14	15	16
21	22	23
28	29	*First Day of Autumn* 30

AUGUST
S	M	T	W	T	F	S
		1	2	3	4	5
6	7	8	9	10	11	12
13	14	15	16	17	18	19
20	21	22	23	24	25	26
27	28	29	30	31		

OCTOBER
S	M	T	W	T	F	S
1	2	3	4	5	6	7
8	9	10	11	12	13	14
15	16	17	18	19	20	21
22	23	24	25	26	27	28
29	30	31				

A FIXED MIND

I'm so stressed today, Lord! I don't like the way this feels. I know I should give these problems to You, but sometimes my fingers are so tightly wound around them that it's hard to unwind them. I feel like You have to pry them from my tightly wedged fingers.

Help me let go, I pray! Give me faith to believe You're bigger than what I'm facing right now, Lord. I don't need much—just a tiny mustard seed. Show me how to keep my mind fixed on You, not the problems. They're swarming around me so fast sometimes that it's hard not to focus on them. I honestly feel lost in a daze of confusion when things get like this. Help!

I'm sorry for the times I've allowed myself to get caught up in the drama of chaotic circumstances, Father. I want to keep my mind fixed on You. Solid. Immovable. You. Only there will I find the peace to make proper decisions. Help me, I pray!

Amen.

GOALS for this MONTH

☐ ....
☐ ....
☐ ....
☐ ....
☐ ....
☐ ....
☐ ....
☐ ....
☐ ....
☐ ....
☐ ....
☐ ....
☐ ....
☐ ....

*You keep him in perfect peace whose mind
is stayed on you, because he trusts in you.*
ISAIAH 26:3 ESV

I won't look to anything—or anyone—else but You, Lord. Answers aren't found in this world. The only true and lasting solution is found in spending time with You and in Your Word.

SUNDAY, September 3

....

....

....

....

MONDAY, September 4   *Labor Day*

....

....

....

....

TUESDAY, September 5

....

....

....

....

WEDNESDAY, September 6

THURSDAY, September 7

FRIDAY, September 8

SATURDAY, September 9

But he said, "What is impossible
with man is possible with God."
LUKE 18:27 ESV

Until I see You face-to-face, Lord, thank You for providing rivers of living water for me to enjoy—right here, right now. Whenever I feel my peace waning, I drink from that pool that never runs dry and I am revived!

SUNDAY, September 10

....
....
....
....

MONDAY, September 11

....
....
....
....

TUESDAY, September 12

....
....
....
....

WEDNESDAY, September 13

....

....

....

....

THURSDAY, September 14

....

....

....

....

FRIDAY, September 15

....

....

....

....

SATURDAY, September 16

....

....

....

....

"Anyone who believes in me may come and drink! For the Scriptures declare, 'Rivers of living water will flow from his heart.'"
JOHN 7:38 NLT

I trust You, Lord. I'll put my faith in the one who owns it all. And I'll remind myself that what I cannot accomplish on my own is Yours to deal with.

SUNDAY, September 17

MONDAY, September 18

TUESDAY, September 19

WEDNESDAY, September 20

THURSDAY, September 21

FRIDAY, September 22

SATURDAY, September 23   *First Day of Autumn*

*I pray that from his glorious, unlimited resources
he will empower you with inner strength
through his Spirit. Then Christ will make
his home in your hearts as you trust in
him. Your roots will grow down into
God's love and keep you strong.*
EPHESIANS 3:16–17 NLT

You're the best guide ever, Lord.
When I acknowledge You in all of my ways,
You really do straighten my paths.

SUNDAY, September 24

MONDAY, September 25

TUESDAY, September 26

WEDNESDAY, September 27

THURSDAY, September 28

FRIDAY, September 29

SATURDAY, September 30

And your ears shall hear a word behind you,
saying, "This is the way, walk in it," when you
turn to the right or when you turn to the left.
Isaiah 30:21 esv

OCTOBER 2023

SUNDAY	MONDAY	TUESDAY	WEDNESDAY
1	2	3	4
8	9 *Columbus Day*	10	11
15	16	17	18
22	23	24	25
29	30	31 *Halloween*	1

THURSDAY	FRIDAY	SATURDAY
5	6	7
12	13	14
19	20	21
26	27	28
2	3	4

STRENGTH FOR THE JOURNEY

I get so weary sometimes, Lord. I feel like I have no strength at all. Even when there's nothing physically wrong with me, sometimes I feel like there is because I can't seem to move at the same pace as before. I wonder if others feel as zapped as I do. They seem to plow forward, regardless.

I just can't. I'm frozen in place. I'm done. There's no moving forward. I'm just too tired.

Then You sweep in, Father, and energize me with Your love. You give me strength for the journey when I need it most. You bring peace, strength, energy, joy, resilience. All of these things are Your free gifts to me, just for spending time with You.

And then I realize that's what's been missing from the equation! I've been so busy working that I forgot to take time with You. No wonder my life is so out of balance, so off-kilter! Thank You for reminding me, as You reminded Martha (Luke 10:41–42), that the better work is just to be with You.

Amen.

GOALS for this MONTH

- [ ] ....
- [ ] ....
- [ ] ....
- [ ] ....
- [ ] ....
- [ ] ....
- [ ] ....
- [ ] ....
- [ ] ....
- [ ] ....
- [ ] ....
- [ ] ....
- [ ] ....
- [ ] ....

*In vain you rise early and stay up
late, toiling for food to eat—for he
grants sleep to those he loves.*

Psalm 127:2 niv

I won't have to wait until I'm in heaven to experience Your goodness, Father. It surrounds me at all times! It encompasses me on every side.

SUNDAY, October 1

....

....

....

....

MONDAY, October 2

....

....

....

....

TUESDAY, October 3

....

....

....

....

WEDNESDAY, October 4

....

....

....

....

THURSDAY, October 5

....

....

....

....

FRIDAY, October 6

....

....

....

....

SATURDAY, October 7

....

....

....

....

*Yet I am confident I will see the LORD's goodness
while I am here in the land of the living.*
PSALM 27:13 NLT

Even though I can't see, I choose to believe,
Lord. Even though I don't hear Your actual
voice, I sense You speaking to my heart,
day in and day out, through every situation.
Because I sense Your nearness, I'm convinced
of Your presence and Your great love.

SUNDAY, October 8

MONDAY, October 9   *Columbus Day*

TUESDAY, October 10

WEDNESDAY, October 11

THURSDAY, October 12

FRIDAY, October 13

SATURDAY, October 14

Though you have not seen him, you love him.
Though you do not now see him, you believe in
him and rejoice with joy that is inexpressible
and filled with glory, obtaining the outcome
of your faith, the salvation of your souls.
1 PETER 1:8–9 ESV

I don't have to search for peace as long as I draw near to You, Lord. I don't need to pull out a treasure map to find joy. Or faith. Or hope. All I have to do is crawl into Your arms for some one-on-one time with my heavenly Father.

SUNDAY, October 15

....

....

....

....

MONDAY, October 16

....

....

....

....

TUESDAY, October 17

....

....

....

....

WEDNESDAY, October 18

THURSDAY, October 19

FRIDAY, October 20

SATURDAY, October 21

Those who know your name put their trust in you, for you, O LORD, have not forsaken those who seek you.
PSALM 9:10 ESV

Lord, thank You today for the godly mentors You have placed in my life! So many times, I've needed the advice or the counsel of someone who really cares, of someone with godly wisdom. And You always manage to send the perfect person, just when the need arises!

SUNDAY, October 22

MONDAY, October 23

TUESDAY, October 24

WEDNESDAY, October 25

THURSDAY, October 26

FRIDAY, October 27

SATURDAY, October 28

*"Blessed is the man who trusts in the LORD,
whose trust is the LORD. He is like a tree planted
by water, that sends out its roots by the
stream, and does not fear when heat
comes, for its leaves remain green, and
is not anxious in the year of drought,
for it does not cease to bear fruit."*
JEREMIAH 17:7–8 ESV

NOVEMBER 2023

SUNDAY	MONDAY	TUESDAY	WEDNESDAY
29	30	31	1
5 *Daylight Saving Time Ends*	6	7 *Election Day*	8
12	13	14	15
19	20	21	22
26	27	28	29

THURSDAY	FRIDAY	SATURDAY
2	3	4
9	10	11 *Veterans Day*
16	17	18
23 *Thanksgiving Day*	24	25
30	1	2

OCTOBER

S	M	T	W	T	F	S
1	2	3	4	5	6	7
8	9	10	11	12	13	14
15	16	17	18	19	20	21
22	23	24	25	26	27	28
29	30	31				

DECEMBER

S	M	T	W	T	F	S
					1	2
3	4	5	6	7	8	9
10	11	12	13	14	15	16
17	18	19	20	21	22	23
24	25	26	27	28	29	30
31						

A LOVING SHEPHERD

You are a good shepherd, Lord. You care for the sheep in Your pasture with such tenderness. No wolf or lion can come near as long as You stand ready, staff in hand. I can trust You, Lord, even when I'm in pastures unknown. You are right there, my Good Shepherd, guarding, protecting, and giving me peace. I know that no enemy can come near as long as You are here. Oh they can try, but none can penetrate Your barrier. I'm safe with You!

Best of all, You make it clear that I belong to You! I'm in the right pasture. You want me. You desire me. You fought hard to win me. So why would I ever wander from the Shepherd who loves me more than anyone else possibly could? No, I'll stay put, Lord, safe in Your care.

Thank You, my Good Shepherd. Amen.

GOALS for this MONTH

- ☐ ....
- ☐ ....
- ☐ ....
- ☐ ....
- ☐ ....
- ☐ ....
- ☐ ....
- ☐ ....
- ☐ ....
- ☐ ....
- ☐ ....
- ☐ ....
- ☐ ....
- ☐ ....

*Know that the LORD, he is God! It is he
who made us, and we are his; we are his
people, and the sheep of his pasture.*
PSALM 100:3 ESV

Your rules guide me, Lord. They're a lovely map laid out for me. They illuminate my path and give light to my eyes. I would be lost without them.

SUNDAY, October 29

....

....

....

....

MONDAY, October 30

....

....

....

....

TUESDAY, October 31   *Halloween*

....

....

....

....

WEDNESDAY, November 1

THURSDAY, November 2

FRIDAY, November 3

SATURDAY, November 4

The precepts of the LORD are right, giving joy
to the heart. The commands of the LORD
are radiant, giving light to the eyes.
PSALM 19:8 NIV

How could I ever walk away from Your love, Father? I won't. Not now, not ever. If I'm ever tempted, please remind me of how deep, how wide, how high, and how vast is Your abounding love! It came from heaven to earth for me!

SUNDAY, November 5 *Daylight Saving Time Ends*

....

....

....

....

MONDAY, November 6

....

....

....

....

TUESDAY, November 7 *Election Day*

....

....

....

....

WEDNESDAY, November 8

THURSDAY, November 9

FRIDAY, November 10

SATURDAY, November 11   *Veterans Day*

*I will not remove from him my steadfast
love or be false to my faithfulness.*
PSALM 89:33 ESV

You're not ruled by the clock, are You, Lord? No,
You have a completely different perspective about
time than I do. I'm mesmerized that You saw my
life before I was even conceived. Long before,
You knew me, You loved me. How remarkable!

SUNDAY, November 12

MONDAY, November 13

TUESDAY, November 14

WEDNESDAY, November 15

THURSDAY, November 16

FRIDAY, November 17

SATURDAY, November 18

I trust in you, O Lᴏʀᴅ; I say, "You are my God."
My times are in your hand; rescue
me from the hand of my enemies
and from my persecutors!
Psᴀʟᴍ 31:14–15 ᴇsᴠ

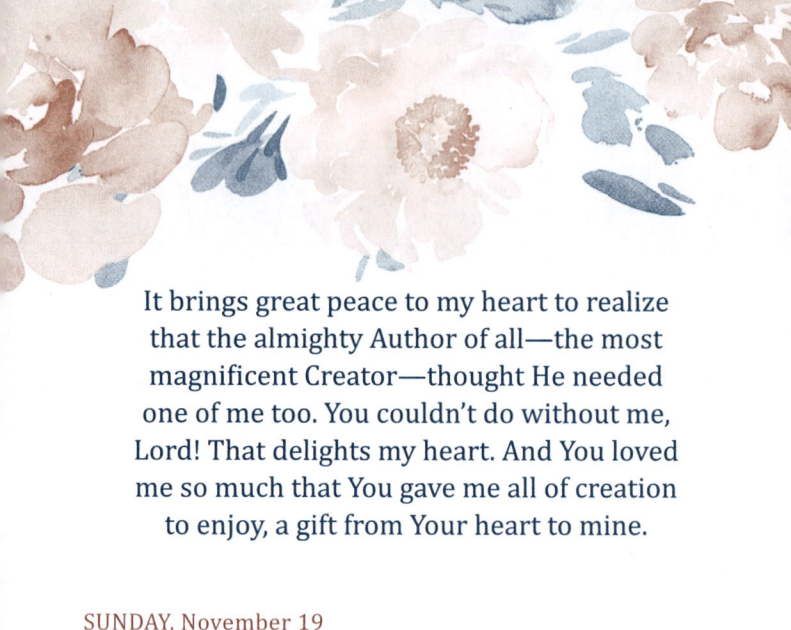

It brings great peace to my heart to realize that the almighty Author of all—the most magnificent Creator—thought He needed one of me too. You couldn't do without me, Lord! That delights my heart. And You loved me so much that You gave me all of creation to enjoy, a gift from Your heart to mine.

SUNDAY, November 19

MONDAY, November 20

TUESDAY, November 21

WEDNESDAY, November 22

THURSDAY, November 23   *Thanksgiving Day*

FRIDAY, November 24

SATURDAY, November 25

*Whatever is good and perfect is a gift coming
down to us from God our Father, who created
all the lights in the heavens. He never
changes or casts a shifting shadow.*
JAMES 1:17 NLT

I'm asking You now, Lord, for more of
You. More of Your Word, Your thoughts,
Your hope, Your peace. Thank You!

SUNDAY, November 26

MONDAY, November 27

TUESDAY, November 28

WEDNESDAY, November 29

....
....
....
....

THURSDAY, November 30

....
....
....
....

FRIDAY, December 1

....
....
....
....

SATURDAY, December 2

....
....
....
....

The decrees of the LORD are firm, and all of them are righteous. They are more precious than gold, than much pure gold; they are sweeter than honey, than honey from the honeycomb.
PSALM 19:9–10 NIV

DECEMBER 2023

SUNDAY	MONDAY	TUESDAY	WEDNESDAY
26	27	28	29
3	4	5	6
10	11	12	13
17	18	19	20
24 *Christmas Eve* / *New Year's Eve* 31	25 *Christmas Day*	26	27

THURSDAY	FRIDAY	SATURDAY
30	1	2
7 *Hanukkah Begins at Sundown*	8	9
14	15	16
21 *First Day of Winter*	22	23
28	29	30

EARLY IN THE MORNING

You speak to me at all times of day, Lord. But there's something so special about the early morning hours as the dawn is peeking through. Before my mind is cluttered with the chaos of the day, I can lean in close to hear Your voice more clearly.

In those moments, when I'm first coming awake, I'm reminded of Your steadfast love, of Your faithfulness to me. There, in that peaceful place, everything seems fresh, new, and possible. Oh, how I love those special morning moments with You!

I can start my day at peace, God, because I hear from You first thing. You nudge me in the right direction, a holy GPS, giving instructions I didn't even know I needed!

I know You want to hear from me first thing too. So I will pour out my heart in the morning hours and give You the best part of my day. Thank You for meeting me there. And thank You for the peace that passes all understanding as I face each precious new day. What a gift!

Amen.

GOALS for this MONTH

- [ ] ....
- [ ] ....
- [ ] ....
- [ ] ....
- [ ] ....
- [ ] ....
- [ ] ....
- [ ] ....
- [ ] ....
- [ ] ....
- [ ] ....
- [ ] ....
- [ ] ....
- [ ] ....

Let me hear in the morning of your steadfast love, for in you I trust. Make me know the way I should go, for to you I lift up my soul.

PSALM 143:8 ESV

Some days I look at the puzzle of my life and
feel like one of the key pieces is missing.
You, Lord, are that missing piece. Put me
back together, I pray. I submit to this lovely
picture You are creating in my life.

SUNDAY, December 3

....
....
....
....

MONDAY, December 4

....
....
....
....

TUESDAY, December 5

....
....
....
....

WEDNESDAY, December 6

THURSDAY, December 7   *Hanukkah Begins at Sundown*

FRIDAY, December 8

SATURDAY, December 9

I am glad I can have complete confidence in you.
2 Corinthians 7:16 niv

As part of Your great plan, You offered me
peace. You said I could cast my anxieties on
You because You care for me. It's obvious,
Lord! You care so much that You gave
Your all. How grateful I am, Father!

SUNDAY, December 10

....

....

....

....

MONDAY, December 11

....

....

....

....

TUESDAY, December 12

....

....

....

....

WEDNESDAY, December 13

THURSDAY, December 14

FRIDAY, December 15

SATURDAY, December 16

Cast all your anxiety on him
because he cares for you.
1 PETER 5:7 NIV

You wouldn't call me to something unless You
equipped me for it, Lord. You must think I'm
ready, or I wouldn't be here! Sure, my knees may
be knocking and my voice might be quivering, but
knowing You've placed me here brings reassurance.

SUNDAY, December 17

MONDAY, December 18

TUESDAY, December 19

WEDNESDAY, December 20

THURSDAY, December 21   *First Day of Winter*

FRIDAY, December 22

SATURDAY, December 23

*All Scripture is breathed out by God and profitable
for teaching, for reproof, for correction,
and for training in righteousness, that
the man of God may be complete,
equipped for every good work.*
2 TIMOTHY 3:16–17 ESV

Lord, no matter how much pain I face, I will
look to You, the one who can bring peace and
hope in my life. There is a path out of this pain.
I will trust You as we walk it, hand in hand.

SUNDAY, December 24   *Christmas Eve*

....

....

....

....

MONDAY, December 25   *Christmas Day*

....

....

....

....

TUESDAY, December 26

....

....

....

....

WEDNESDAY, December 27

....

....

....

....

THURSDAY, December 28

....

....

....

....

FRIDAY, December 29

....

....

....

....

SATURDAY, December 30

....

....

....

....

For everyone who has been born of God overcomes the world. And this is the victory that has overcome the world—our faith.
1 John 5:4 esv

JANUARY 2024

SUNDAY	MONDAY	TUESDAY	WEDNESDAY
31	1 *New Year's Day*	2	3
7	8	9	10
14	15 *Martin Luther King Jr. Day*	16	17
21	22	23	24
28	29	30	31

THURSDAY	FRIDAY	SATURDAY
4	5	6
11	12	13
18	19	20
25	26	27
1	2	3

DECEMBER

S	M	T	W	T	F	S
					1	2
3	4	5	6	7	8	9
10	11	12	13	14	15	16
17	18	19	20	21	22	23
24	25	26	27	28	29	30
31						

FEBRUARY

S	M	T	W	T	F	S
				1	2	3
4	5	6	7	8	9	10
11	12	13	14	15	16	17
18	19	20	21	22	23	24
25	26	27	28	29		

THE MISSING INGREDIENT

I sense it every day, Lord. The greatness of Your vast love sweeps over me, transforming me with Your goodness. Though I don't deserve it, You pour it out, like water from a wash basin, a beautiful flow to cleanse even the grimiest parts of me, the bits I strive to hide from all.

Oh, but I could never hide from You, Lord! In the safety of Your care, I'm reminded of the great depth of Your love—of its width, its breadth, its height. When I'm there, in that precious place with You, nothing else matters. I don't try to make sense of it, to analyze it. Instead, I soak in it, a sponge withered and dry until the moment Your touch changes everything.

Oh, how I praise You! You complete me with this vast love. It's the missing ingredient, the hole filler, the power giver, the light for my path. Show me how to love as You do so that others might experience this same life-giving peace.

Amen.

GOALS for this MONTH

- [ ] ....
- [ ] ....
- [ ] ....
- [ ] ....
- [ ] ....
- [ ] ....
- [ ] ....
- [ ] ....
- [ ] ....
- [ ] ....
- [ ] ....
- [ ] ....
- [ ] ....

*And may you have the power to understand,
as all God's people should, how wide, how
long, how high, and how deep his love is. May
you experience the love of Christ, though it
is too great to understand fully. Then you
will be made complete with all the fullness
of life and power that comes from God.*

EPHESIANS 3:18–19 NLT

I open myself up to Your river, Father.
Take the cracked, parched places of my heart.
Take every unsettled feeling, every hurt, every
misunderstanding. Pour Your peace over my
wounded soul. Refresh me anew, I pray.

SUNDAY, December 31   *New Year's Eve*

....

....

....

....

MONDAY, January 1   *New Year's Day*

....

....

....

....

TUESDAY, January 2

....

....

....

....

WEDNESDAY, January 3

THURSDAY, January 4

FRIDAY, January 5

SATURDAY, January 6

Now the earth was formless and empty, darkness was over the surface of the deep, and the Spirit of God was hovering over the waters.
GENESIS 1:2 NIV

Lord, there's really only one place I can put my trust—in You. During tumultuous times I will be of good courage as I place my trust solely where it belongs—on the only one who has never let me down! Thank You for that, Lord.

SUNDAY, January 7

....

....

....

....

MONDAY, January 8

....

....

....

TUESDAY, January 9

....

....

....

....

WEDNESDAY, January 10

THURSDAY, January 11

FRIDAY, January 12

SATURDAY, January 13

*We are always of good courage. We know
that while we are at home in the body
we are away from the Lord, for we
walk by faith, not by sight.*
2 Corinthians 5:6–7 esv

Because You've chosen me to be Yours forever and I've believed on Your name, we'll have a relationship that transcends time. I'll never understand it, Lord, but maybe I wasn't meant to. Instead, I'll just enjoy my "forever" time with You.

SUNDAY, January 14

....
....
....
....

MONDAY, January 15·   *Martin Luther King Jr. Day*

....
....
....
....

TUESDAY, January 16

....
....
....
....

WEDNESDAY, January 17

....
....
....
....

THURSDAY, January 18

....
....
....
....

FRIDAY, January 19

....
....
....
....

SATURDAY, January 20

....
....
....
....

I write these things to you who believe in the name of the Son of God, that you may know that you have eternal life.
1 JOHN 5:13 ESV

In You my heart finally found its resting place, Lord.
I am Yours forever. I am home forever. Here, I am
known. You know everything about me—when I sit,
when I rise, even what I'm thinking. Oh, how lovely,
to be home at last with the one who loves me most.

SUNDAY, January 21

MONDAY, January 22

TUESDAY, January 23

WEDNESDAY, January 24

....

....

....

....

THURSDAY, January 25

....

....

....

....

FRIDAY, January 26

....

....

....

....

SATURDAY, January 27

....

....

....

....

You know when I sit and when I rise;
you perceive my thoughts from afar.
PSALM 139:2 NIV

FEBRUARY 2024

SUNDAY	MONDAY	TUESDAY	WEDNESDAY
28	29	30	31
4	5	6	7
11	12	13	14 *Valentine's Day* *Ash Wednesday*
18	19 *Presidents' Day*	20	21
25	26	27	28

THURSDAY	FRIDAY	SATURDAY
1	2	3
8	9	10
15	16	17
22	23	24
29 *Leap Day*	1	2

JANUARY

S	M	T	W	T	F	S
	1	2	3	4	5	6
7	8	9	10	11	12	13
14	15	16	17	18	19	20
21	22	23	24	25	26	27
28	29	30	31			

MARCH

S	M	T	W	T	F	S
					1	2
3	4	5	6	7	8	9
10	11	12	13	14	15	16
17	18	19	20	21	22	23
24	25	26	27	28	29	30
31						

RELAX AND ENJOY

It's so ironic, Lord, that I should have to work my way into resting. It would be easier if I could just relax and enjoy the peace of the Sabbath. But I'm inclined to work and to stay active. Slowing down and having quiet time goes against my nature.

You must have known we would be like this! That's why there are so many references to Sabbath rest in Your Word. You knew that we would require teaching, and that resting would require effort on our part.

Break the tendency in me to work around the clock, Lord! Teach me how to enter into Your rest, I pray. I want to be refreshed and invigorated for the journey ahead, and that can only happen as I lay down the busyness and draw near to You.

Amen.

GOALS for this MONTH

- [ ] ....
- [ ] ....
- [ ] ....
- [ ] ....
- [ ] ....
- [ ] ....
- [ ] ....
- [ ] ....
- [ ] ....
- [ ] ....
- [ ] ....
- [ ] ....
- [ ] ....

There remains, then, a Sabbath-rest for the people of God; for anyone who enters God's rest also rests from their works, just as God did from his. Let us, therefore, make every effort to enter that rest, so that no one will perish by following their example of disobedience.

HEBREWS 4:9–11 NIV

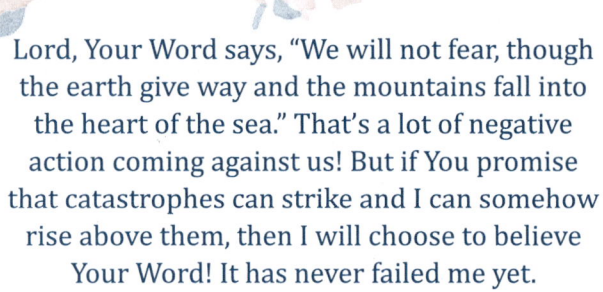

Lord, Your Word says, "We will not fear, though the earth give way and the mountains fall into the heart of the sea." That's a lot of negative action coming against us! But if You promise that catastrophes can strike and I can somehow rise above them, then I will choose to believe Your Word! It has never failed me yet.

SUNDAY, January 28

....

....

....

....

MONDAY, January 29

....

....

....

....

TUESDAY, January 30

....

....

....

....

WEDNESDAY, January 31

....

....

....

....

THURSDAY, February 1

....

....

....

....

FRIDAY, February 2

....

....

....

....

SATURDAY, February 3

....

....

....

....

Therefore we will not fear, though the earth give way and the mountains fall into the heart of the sea.
PSALM 46:2 NIV

Heavenly Father, You've shown me how to walk
in peace even through difficult situations. You've
given me joy for the journey. You've taught
me that I can rise above my circumstances.
You've blessed me beyond belief!

SUNDAY, February 4

....
....
....
....

MONDAY, February 5

....
....
....
....

TUESDAY, February 6

....
....
....
....

WEDNESDAY, February 7

THURSDAY, February 8

FRIDAY, February 9

SATURDAY, February 10

*Moreover, it is required of stewards
that they be found faithful.*
1 CORINTHIANS 4:2 ESV

Right now I hand over my anxieties, my worries, my desires to You, Lord, that I might walk in full and abundant peace. No looking back. No stressing about tomorrow. I want the joy that only You can bring and the hope that a stress-free day will offer.

SUNDAY, February 11

MONDAY, February 12

TUESDAY, February 13

WEDNESDAY, February 14 *Valentine's Day, Ash Wednesday*

THURSDAY, February 15

FRIDAY, February 16

SATURDAY, February 17

May the God of hope fill you with all joy and peace in believing, so that by the power of the Holy Spirit you may abound in hope.
ROMANS 15:13 ESV

Lord, when trouble comes, I stand in peace
and tranquility, trusting You—the one who
lifts me above the battle, the one who goes
before me, the one with the master plan.

SUNDAY, February 18

....

....

....

....

MONDAY, February 19   *Presidents' Day*

....

....

....

....

TUESDAY, February 20

....

....

....

....

WEDNESDAY, February 21

....

....

....

....

THURSDAY, February 22

....

....

....

....

FRIDAY, February 23

....

....

....

....

SATURDAY, February 24

....

....

....

....

*When I am afraid, I put my trust in you. In God,
whose word I praise—in God I trust and am
not afraid. What can mere mortals do to me?
All day long they twist my words; all their
schemes are for my ruin. . . . Because of
their wickedness do not let them escape;
in your anger, God, bring the nations down.*
PSALM 56:3–5, 7 NIV

I praise You, Lord! I celebrate this precious
life You've given me, and I give You all of
my adoration. You are my King of kings, my
Lord of lords, my everything. Worthy are
You to be praised, today and every day!

SUNDAY, February 25

MONDAY, February 26

TUESDAY, February 27

WEDNESDAY, February 28

....
....
....
....

THURSDAY, February 29   *Leap Day*

....
....
....
....

FRIDAY, March 1

....
....
....
....

SATURDAY, March 2

....
....
....
....

*Trust in him at all times, you people; pour out
your hearts to him, for God is our refuge.*
PSALM 62:8 NIV

MARCH 2024

SUNDAY	MONDAY	TUESDAY	WEDNESDAY
25	26	27	28
3	4	5	6
10 *Daylight Saving Time Begins*	11	12	13
17 *St. Patrick's Day*	18	19 *First Day of Spring*	20
24 *Palm Sunday* / *Easter Sunday* 31	25	26	27

THURSDAY	FRIDAY	SATURDAY
29	1	2
7	8	9
14	15	16
21	22	23
28	29 *Good Friday*	30

FATHER, I COME

Lord, You call me to abide with You, to dwell daily, hourly, even by the moment, with You. You've grafted me in and want me to stick close. For that to happen, I have to shift my attention from the (many!) things that are calling my name—bills, work, pets, a messy kitchen. My goodness, the distractions are real, Lord!

I confess, sometimes it's hard for me just to be. I would rather be up and doing, tending to the obvious things that demand my attention. I forget that they can wait, and that spending time with You is the most important part of each day.

During the abiding moments, You fill my heart with such peace, joy, and tranquility. Why would I put that off? I can't find those things when I'm rushing around in a frenzy. I don't sense them when my eyes are otherwise focused. But when I take the time to abide with You, peace like a river washes over me.

How grateful I am for that abiding peace today. Father, I come!

Amen.

GOALS for this MONTH

- ☐ ....
- ☐ ....
- ☐ ....
- ☐ ....
- ☐ ....
- ☐ ....
- ☐ ....
- ☐ ....
- ☐ ....
- ☐ ....
- ☐ ....
- ☐ ....
- ☐ ....

It is better to take refuge in the
Lord than to trust in man.
Psalm 118:8 esv

Today, Lord, I choose to reestablish my trust in You. May I never forget. May I never lose hope in the only one who has never let me down.

SUNDAY, March 3

MONDAY, March 4

TUESDAY, March 5

WEDNESDAY, March 6

THURSDAY, March 7

FRIDAY, March 8

SATURDAY, March 9

*The Lord replied, "I will make all my goodness
pass before you, and I will call out my name,
Yahweh, before you. For I will show mercy
to anyone I choose, and I will show
compassion to anyone I choose."*
EXODUS 33:19 NLT

You're an amazing warrior, Lord! May I never forget. May I learn from how You fight. And may each victory serve as a reminder that, even in the heat of war, I don't have to be afraid. Even when the enemy is staring me in the face, I can be at peace, knowing that God is on my side.

SUNDAY, March 10   *Daylight Saving Time Begins*

....
....
....
....

MONDAY, March 11

....
....
....
....

TUESDAY, March 12

....
....
....
....

WEDNESDAY, March 13

THURSDAY, March 14

FRIDAY, March 15

SATURDAY, March 16

*"Take my yoke upon you and learn from me,
for I am gentle and humble in heart, and
you will find rest for your souls."*
MATTHEW 11:29 NIV

Lord, You have good pastures for me, lush and green. So when You cause me to be still and spend time there, I will not argue. It is a privilege to lie in green pastures with the one who knows me best and loves me most.

SUNDAY, March 17   *St. Patrick's Day*

....

....

....

....

MONDAY, March 18

....

....

....

....

TUESDAY, March 19   *First Day of Spring*

....

....

....

....

WEDNESDAY, March 20

....

....

....

THURSDAY, March 21

....

....

....

FRIDAY, March 22

....

....

....

SATURDAY, March 23

....

....

....

*Do you not know? Have you not heard? The
Lord is the everlasting God, the Creator of the
ends of the earth. He will not grow tired or
weary, and his understanding no one can
fathom. He gives strength to the weary
and increases the power of the weak.*
Isaiah 40:28–29 niv

Heavenly Father, You timed my arrival perfectly. You have great things planned for me. I can trust Your plans and Your perfect timing. I was born in the right year, the right month, the right place, and the right situation to accomplish all that You have for me.

SUNDAY, March 24 *Palm Sunday*

....

....

....

....

MONDAY, March 25

....

....

....

....

TUESDAY, March 26

....

....

....

....

WEDNESDAY, March 27

THURSDAY, March 28

FRIDAY, March 29   *Good Friday*

SATURDAY, March 30

*"For if you remain silent at this time,
relief and deliverance for the Jews will
arise from another place, but you and your
father's family will perish. And who knows
but that you have come to your royal
position for such a time as this?"*
ESTHER 4:14 NIV

APRIL 2024

SUNDAY	MONDAY	TUESDAY	WEDNESDAY
31	1	2	3
7	8	9	10
14	15	16	17
21	22 *Passover Begins at Sundown*	23	24
28	29	30	1

THURSDAY	FRIDAY	SATURDAY
4	5	6
11	12	13
18	19	20
25	26	27
2	3	4

MARCH

S	M	T	W	T	F	S
					1	2
3	4	5	6	7	8	9
10	11	12	13	14	15	16
17	18	19	20	21	22	23
24	25	26	27	28	29	30
31						

MAY

S	M	T	W	T	F	S
			1	2	3	4
5	6	7	8	9	10	11
12	13	14	15	16	17	18
19	20	21	22	23	24	25
26	27	28	29	30	31	

CALMING THE STORMS

At times it feels like there's a volcano in my heart, Lord. I can feel it rumbling, rumbling, rumbling, threatening to erupt. At any moment now, it's going to blow and the devastation will be shocking. Devastating. I'm going to take out whole villages with the eruption, I'm afraid. Or at least tear down those I love.

That's my fear, anyway. I can see the potential for disaster as my insides tremble like lava.

What can squelch the volcano? What can tamp down the rumble, put out the fire? Only You, Lord. When I'm stirred up like this, You can step in and rebuke the winds and the waves. You can calm the tempest. You can, with one word, push the lava back down into the volcano. In fact, You can cool things down to the point where that volcano never blows again.

I need Your intervention, Father. Calm the storms in me, I pray. Bring peace to this tumultuous heart. Oh, how I need You!

Amen.

GOALS for this MONTH

- [ ] ....
- [ ] ....
- [ ] ....
- [ ] ....
- [ ] ....
- [ ] ....
- [ ] ....
- [ ] ....
- [ ] ....
- [ ] ....
- [ ] ....
- [ ] ....
- [ ] ....
- [ ] ....

*He replied, "You of little faith, why are
you so afraid?" Then he got up and
rebuked the winds and the waves,
and it was completely calm.*

MATTHEW 8:26 NIV

Father, You're a God of positivity. The glass
isn't just half full with You. It's overflowing!
It's running down the sides, spilling
over onto others around me.

SUNDAY, March 31   *Easter Sunday*

....

....

....

....

MONDAY, April 1

....

....

....

....

TUESDAY, April 2

....

....

....

....

WEDNESDAY, April 3

THURSDAY, April 4

FRIDAY, April 5

SATURDAY, April 6

Search me, God, and know my heart;
test me and know my anxious thoughts.
PSALM 139:23 NIV

Heavenly Father, I'll obey You because I love You. And because You love me, You'll continue to pour out blessings that go above anything I could ask or think. You hold nothing back from me. I will hold nothing back from You. Thank You for Your abundance, Lord!

SUNDAY, April 7

MONDAY, April 8

TUESDAY, April 9

WEDNESDAY, April 10

THURSDAY, April 11

FRIDAY, April 12

SATURDAY, April 13

For the LORD God is our sun and our shield. He gives us grace and glory. The LORD will withhold no good thing from those who do what is right.
PSALM 84:11 NLT

God, there's nothing in my life that You are unaware of. You love me deeply! You always have. Knowing that my Creator was on the job long before I existed gives me a tremendous sense of peace.

SUNDAY, April 14

....

....

....

....

MONDAY, April 15

....

....

....

....

TUESDAY, April 16

....

....

....

....

WEDNESDAY, April 17

THURSDAY, April 18

FRIDAY, April 19

SATURDAY, April 20

"Before I formed you in the womb I knew you,
and before you were born I consecrated you;
I appointed you a prophet to the nations."
JEREMIAH 1:5 ESV

What joy to know that I always fit in with You, Father. Knowing that I don't have to try brings me great peace. With You, I can simply be who You created me to be. I will come to You, and You will never turn me away—even when I'm my truest self. How grateful I am!

SUNDAY, April 21

MONDAY, April 22 *Passover Begins at Sundown*

TUESDAY, April 23

WEDNESDAY, April 24

THURSDAY, April 25

FRIDAY, April 26

SATURDAY, April 27

*"All those the Father gives me will
come to me, and whoever comes
to me I will never drive away."*
JOHN 6:37 NIV

MAY 2024

SUNDAY	MONDAY	TUESDAY	WEDNESDAY
28	29	30	1
5	6	7	8
12	13	14	15
Mother's Day			
19	20	21	22
26	27	28	29
	Memorial Day		

THURSDAY	FRIDAY	SATURDAY
2	3	4
National Day of Prayer		
9	10	11
16	17	18
23	24	25
30	31	1

APRIL

S	M	T	W	T	F	S
	1	2	3	4	5	6
7	8	9	10	11	12	13
14	15	16	17	18	19	20
21	22	23	24	25	26	27
28	29	30				

JUNE

S	M	T	W	T	F	S
						1
2	3	4	5	6	7	8
9	10	11	12	13	14	15
16	17	18	19	20	21	22
23	24	25	26	27	28	29
30						

SHOWER THE GARDEN OF MY HEART

Sometimes I feel like my heart is a garden, Lord, and You are the Master Gardener. You tend to the weeds that grow up—the ones that threaten to choke out any signs of life. And You plant my roots in You down deep, so that I can blossom and grow, despite any changes in the conditions around me. (And do they ever change from day to day!)

I'm sorry for the times I've just skimmed the surface of our relationship. When I allow that to happen, I grow weak in faith. I lose my peace and wonder why. But I know why! It's because I've secluded myself far from You. I don't allow You to till the soil of my heart. I don't let my roots run deep, as I should.

But those days are behind me now! Today I invite You back in to tend to this dry, cracked soil. Nurture, saturate, and tend to me as only You can, Lord. Soften the soil so that my roots can go way, way down to the deepest places with You, I pray.

Amen.

GOALS for this MONTH

- [ ] ....
- [ ] ....
- [ ] ....
- [ ] ....
- [ ] ....
- [ ] ....
- [ ] ....
- [ ] ....
- [ ] ....
- [ ] ....
- [ ] ....
- [ ] ....
- [ ] ....
- [ ] ....

*The LORD is good to everyone. He showers
compassion on all his creation.*
PSALM 145:9 NLT

You are a God of peace, not chaos. So when this whirling, swirling world threatens to knock me off my game, I will stand firm, look the enemy in the eye, and say, "Not today, devil!"

SUNDAY, April 28

....
....
....
....

MONDAY, April 29

....
....
....
....

TUESDAY, April 30

....
....
....
....

WEDNESDAY, May 1

....

....

....

....

THURSDAY, May 2   *National Day of Prayer*

....

....

....

....

FRIDAY, May 3

....

....

....

....

SATURDAY, May 4

....

....

....

....

For God is not a God of confusion but of peace.
1 Corinthians 14:33 esv

God, Your Word says that You are at the center when two or three are gathered in Your name. That's obvious to me as I hang out with other believers. I sense Your presence. I'm pretty sure they sense it too. We're a force to be reckoned with when we invite You to the party, Lord!

SUNDAY, May 5

....

....

....

....

MONDAY, May 6

....

....

....

TUESDAY, May 7

....

....

....

....

WEDNESDAY, May 8

THURSDAY, May 9

FRIDAY, May 10

SATURDAY, May 11

*"For where two or three are gathered in
my name, there am I among them."*
MATTHEW 18:20 ESV

I must stay focused, Lord. How I long for an
undivided heart, one that is fully devoted to
You. No distractions. No temptations. Only
You, Jesus. Nothing can ever compare, and
certainly nothing can bring peace as You
do. Give me an undivided heart, I pray.

SUNDAY, May 12   *Mother's Day*

MONDAY, May 13

TUESDAY, May 14

WEDNESDAY, May 15

THURSDAY, May 16

FRIDAY, May 17

SATURDAY, May 18

Teach me your way, LORD, that I may rely on your faithfulness; give me an undivided heart, that I may fear your name.
PSALM 86:11 NIV

Thank You, Lord, for the reminder that I was never meant to carry it all. Your Word tells me to lay aside every weight, not pick it up! Next time I'm about to reach for something that I'm not meant to lift, stop me in my tracks, I pray.

SUNDAY, May 19

MONDAY, May 20

TUESDAY, May 21

WEDNESDAY, May 22

THURSDAY, May 23

FRIDAY, May 24

SATURDAY, May 25

*Therefore, since we are surrounded by so great
a cloud of witnesses, let us also lay aside
every weight, and sin which clings so
closely, and let us run with endurance
the race that is set before us.*
HEBREWS 12:1 ESV

Heavenly Father, my encounters with You can be life altering when I worship in spirit and in truth. It's not just head knowledge I need; it's heart knowledge! It's Spirit-breathed knowledge! And all of that can be mine for the taking in my daily encounters with You if I just ask.

SUNDAY, May 26

MONDAY, May 27   *Memorial Day*

TUESDAY, May 28

WEDNESDAY, May 29

THURSDAY, May 30

FRIDAY, May 31

SATURDAY, June 1

"The hour is coming, and is now here, when the true worshipers will worship the Father in spirit and truth, for the Father is seeking such people to worship him."
JOHN 4:23 ESV

JUNE 2024

SUNDAY	MONDAY	TUESDAY	WEDNESDAY
26	27	28	29
2	3	4	5
9	10	11	12
16	17	18	19
Father's Day			
23	24	25	26
30			

THURSDAY	FRIDAY	SATURDAY
30	31	1
6	7	8
13	14	15
	Flag Day	
20	21	22
First Day of Summer		
27	28	29

MAY

S	M	T	W	T	F	S
				1	2	3	4
5	6	7	8	9	10	11
12	13	14	15	16	17	18
19	20	21	22	23	24	25
26	27	28	29	30	31	

JULY

S	M	T	W	T	F	S
	1	2	3	4	5	6
7	8	9	10	11	12	13
14	15	16	17	18	19	20
21	22	23	24	25	26	27
28	29	30	31			

FOUND FAITHFUL

Life seems to run in seasons, Lord. I have seasons of lack, seasons of plenty. Seasons when life plods along at a slow rate, and seasons when everything seems to be whizzing by me.

There are seasons when I trust You implicitly and other seasons where I hide myself away, cowering in fear. I forget that You're trustworthy, and I cringe in distress and utter helplessness.

Help me to discern the seasons, Father, so that I can live a consistent, peaceful life no matter what's swirling around me. I will not be controlled by the shifting winds—the hot, the cold, the tepid, the balmy—because I know who controls the seasons. You're in control of them all, just as You are in control of my heart. May I be found faithful in trusting You, Lord!

Amen.

GOALS for this MONTH

- [ ] ....
- [ ] ....
- [ ] ....
- [ ] ....
- [ ] ....
- [ ] ....
- [ ] ....
- [ ] ....
- [ ] ....
- [ ] ....
- [ ] ....
- [ ] ....

*"Who then is the faithful and wise servant,
whom his master has set over his household,
to give them their food at the proper time?
Blessed is that servant whom his master will
find so doing when he comes. Truly, I say to
you, he will set him over all his possessions."*
MATTHEW 24:45–47 ESV

I can't think of one mediocre thing that You ever created, Lord. Every single creation is spectacular, down to the finest detail. From cumulus clouds floating in the sky above to tiny grasshoppers moving beneath my feet! You thought of literally everything.

SUNDAY, June 2

....

....

....

....

MONDAY, June 3

....

....

....

TUESDAY, June 4

....

....

....

....

WEDNESDAY, June 5

....

....

....

....

THURSDAY, June 6

....

....

....

....

FRIDAY, June 7

....

....

....

....

SATURDAY, June 8

....

....

....

....

Since everything God created is good, we should not reject any of it but receive it with thanks.
1 TIMOTHY 4:4 NLT

What assurance I have to know You are covering me, Lord! You are so good to me! What a blessing to know that I will be pursued all the days of my life by Your goodness and Your mercy, and that I can live in Your house forever. I'm so encouraged by You, Lord!

SUNDAY, June 9

MONDAY, June 10

TUESDAY, June 11

WEDNESDAY, June 12

THURSDAY, June 13

FRIDAY, June 14   *Flag Day*

SATURDAY, June 15

Surely goodness and mercy shall follow me
all the days of my life: and I will dwell
in the house of the Lord for ever.
Psalm 23:6 kjv

Your ways are too lofty for me, Father! Your thoughts too high. But I will stand in awe as I consider Your great works, remembering that You cared enough to create me too. I have great peace, knowing that such a profound Creator is caring for me.

SUNDAY, June 16   *Father's Day*

MONDAY, June 17

TUESDAY, June 18

WEDNESDAY, June 19

THURSDAY, June 20   *First Day of Summer*

FRIDAY, June 21

SATURDAY, June 22

For you make me glad by your deeds, Lord;
I sing for joy at what your hands have
done. How great are your works, Lord,
how profound your thoughts!
Psalm 92:4–5 niv

Lord. I can live at peace knowing that the very one who walked out of the tomb is in complete control of my life. Battles will be waged against me. I see what the enemy of my soul is up to. But I'm the daughter of God. What peace, placing my trust in a risen Savior like You!

SUNDAY, June 23

....

....

....

....

MONDAY, June 24

....

....

....

....

TUESDAY, June 25

....

....

....

....

WEDNESDAY, June 26

....
....
....
....

THURSDAY, June 27

....
....
....
....

FRIDAY, June 28

....
....
....
....

SATURDAY, June 29

....
....
....
....

*Though an army besiege me, my heart will
not fear; though war break out against
me, even then I will be confident.*
PSALM 27:3 NIV

JULY 2024

SUNDAY	MONDAY	TUESDAY	WEDNESDAY
30	1	2	3
7	8	9	10
14	15	16	17
21	22	23	24
28	29	30	31

THURSDAY	FRIDAY	SATURDAY
4 *Independence Day*	5	6
11	12	13
18	19	20
25	26	27
1	2	3

JUNE

S	M	T	W	T	F	S
						1
2	3	4	5	6	7	8
9	10	11	12	13	14	15
16	17	18	19	20	21	22
23	24	25	26	27	28	29
30						

AUGUST

S	M	T	W	T	F	S
				1	2	3
4	5	6	7	8	9	10
11	12	13	14	15	16	17
18	19	20	21	22	23	24
25	26	27	28	29	30	31

HIS GOODNESS

I hear the birds singing their joy song in the tree just beyond my front window. High above the turmoil of this world, they reside in their nest, safely tucked away, free to sing to their hearts' content.

How I long to be at peace as they are! How I desire to be lifted above and beyond the turmoil of my day-to-day existence.

Your Word says that You are good and You do only good. How often I forget that! I stop singing my birdsong because I'm weighted down with the cares of life. I forget that You have a handle on everything. Seal my heart with that truth. May I never forget that You created me to soar above those circumstances, much as the carefree birds fly back to their nest.

Today I choose to spend my hours in flight, set free because of Your great love.

Amen.

GOALS for this MONTH

- [ ] ....
- [ ] ....
- [ ] ....
- [ ] ....
- [ ] ....
- [ ] ....
- [ ] ....
- [ ] ....
- [ ] ....
- [ ] ....
- [ ] ....
- [ ] ....
- [ ] ....
- [ ] ....

You are good and do only good;
teach me your decrees.
PSALM 119:68 NLT

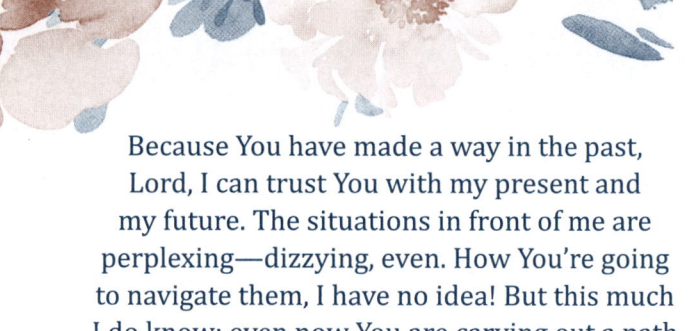

Because You have made a way in the past,
Lord, I can trust You with my present and
my future. The situations in front of me are
perplexing—dizzying, even. How You're going
to navigate them, I have no idea! But this much
I do know: even now You are carving out a path
in the desert, a way through the wilderness.

SUNDAY, June 30

MONDAY, July 1

TUESDAY, July 2

WEDNESDAY, July 3

THURSDAY, July 4   *Independence Day*

FRIDAY, July 5

SATURDAY, July 6

*No temptation has overtaken you that is not common
to man. God is faithful, and he will not let you
be tempted beyond your ability, but with the
temptation he will also provide the way of
escape, that you may be able to endure it.*
1 Corinthians 10:13 esv

You are the God of light! You're like a high-beam flashlight guiding my way. You know what's coming around the bend, and You are my radiant Lord, taking hold of my hand and leading me past the shadows into Your glorious presence.

SUNDAY, July 7

....
....
....
....

MONDAY, July 8

....
....
....

TUESDAY, July 9

....
....
....
....

WEDNESDAY, July 10

THURSDAY, July 11

FRIDAY, July 12

SATURDAY, July 13

Light shines on the righteous and joy on the upright in heart.
PSALM 97:11 NIV

Heavenly Father, I have such peace today,
not despite the struggles I've been through,
but *because* of them. Because I have struggled
and overcome, I have reason to celebrate!

SUNDAY, July 14

MONDAY, July 15

TUESDAY, July 16

WEDNESDAY, July 17

THURSDAY, July 18

FRIDAY, July 19

SATURDAY, July 20

Everyone born of God overcomes the world. This is the victory that has overcome the world, even our faith.
1 JOHN 5:4 NIV

Your ways really are best, Lord. They bring
peace to my soul and health to my
weary body! Thank You for teaching
me how to rest secure in You.

SUNDAY, July 21

....

....

....

....

MONDAY, July 22

....

....

....

....

TUESDAY, July 23

....

....

....

....

WEDNESDAY, July 24

THURSDAY, July 25

FRIDAY, July 26

SATURDAY, July 27

Therefore my heart is glad and my tongue rejoices; my body also will rest secure.
PSALM 16:9 NIV

AUGUST 2024

SUNDAY	MONDAY	TUESDAY	WEDNESDAY
28	29	30	31
4	5	6	7
11	12	13	14
18	19	20	21
25	26	27	28

THURSDAY	FRIDAY	SATURDAY
1	2	3
8	9	10
15	16	17
22	23	24
29	30	31

JULY

S	M	T	W	T	F	S
	1	2	3	4	5	6
7	8	9	10	11	12	13
14	15	16	17	18	19	20
21	22	23	24	25	26	27
28	29	30	31			

SEPTEMBER

S	M	T	W	T	F	S
1	2	3	4	5	6	7
8	9	10	11	12	13	14
15	16	17	18	19	20	21
22	23	24	25	26	27	28
29	30					

DWELL IN SAFETY

You see me, Lord. You see my tears in the night. You see my struggles in the daytime. You see the apprehension when I'm facing something uncertain. You see the joy when I'm with those I love. You see the troubles that are yet to come, and You see the victories that are ahead. I can trust You, Lord, and I can have peace, because I know that You have 20-20 supernatural vision.

Best of all, You see me in the night, during those hours when I'm tossing and turning, fretting over this or that. When I'm nervous about every little thing that goes bump in the night. When I'm losing sleep over the troubles of the day.

Yes, You see me in the night (with Your terrific night vision!), and You comfort me. You bring peace. You cause me to dwell in safety. Only when I feel safe and secure can I (finally!) roll over and go to sleep.

What a blessing to be safely cared for by You, Lord. Amen.

GOALS for this MONTH

- [ ] ....
- [ ] ....
- [ ] ....
- [ ] ....
- [ ] ....
- [ ] ....
- [ ] ....
- [ ] ....
- [ ] ....
- [ ] ....
- [ ] ....
- [ ] ....
- [ ] ....
- [ ] ....

*In peace I will both lie
down and sleep; for you alone,
O LORD, make me dwell in safety.*

PSALM 4:8 ESV

Lord, You leave behind zero messes. If You fluctuated and changed the way I am prone to do, chaos would abound in the universe. But You? You never change, Lord. You're dressed in righteousness, peace, and joy every day all day, year in and year out.

SUNDAY, July 28

....

....

....

....

MONDAY, July 29

....

....

....

....

TUESDAY, July 30

....

....

....

....

WEDNESDAY, July 31

THURSDAY, August 1

FRIDAY, August 2

SATURDAY, August 3

"I the LORD do not change; therefore you,
O children of Jacob, are not consumed."
MALACHI 3:6 ESV

You've given me a merry heart, Lord!
All day long this joyful heart of mine is
on the verge of breaking into song. You've
given me so much to celebrate, after all!

SUNDAY, August 4

MONDAY, August 5

TUESDAY, August 6

WEDNESDAY, August 7

THURSDAY, August 8

FRIDAY, August 9

SATURDAY, August 10

My heart, O God, is steadfast; I will sing and make music with all my soul.
PSALM 108:1 NIV

Thank You for caring so much about my journey, Father. Thank You for taking the time to straighten things out when they're lopsided or crooked. (I've given You plenty of opportunities, haven't I, Lord?) Oh, how You love me!

SUNDAY, August 11

....
....
....
....

MONDAY, August 12

....
....
....
....

TUESDAY, August 13

....
....
....
....

WEDNESDAY, August 14

THURSDAY, August 15

FRIDAY, August 16

SATURDAY, August 17

In all your ways submit to him, and he will make your paths straight.
PROVERBS 3:6 NIV

My heart is set free under Your amazing grace, Lord. Sin has no place in my life and will certainly not control me any longer. Thank You for that revelation!

SUNDAY, August 18

....

....

....

....

MONDAY, August 19

....

....

....

....

TUESDAY, August 20

....

....

....

....

WEDNESDAY, August 21

....

....

....

....

THURSDAY, August 22

....

....

....

....

FRIDAY, August 23

....

....

....

....

SATURDAY, August 24

....

....

....

....

For sin will have no dominion over you,
since you are not under law but under grace.
ROMANS 6:14 ESV

Heavenly Father, I'm so glad I can put my trust in You and not in human wisdom. Eternal justice will prevail. I don't know when, but I do know how. You, Lord, will bring it to pass. And it will shine in radiant splendor.

SUNDAY, August 25

....

....

....

....

MONDAY, August 26

....

....

....

....

TUESDAY, August 27

....

....

....

....

WEDNESDAY, August 28

....

....

....

....

THURSDAY, August 29

....

....

....

....

FRIDAY, August 30

....

....

....

....

SATURDAY, August 31

....

....

....

....

Commit your way to the LORD; trust in him, and he will act. He will bring forth your righteousness as the light, and your justice as the noonday.
PSALM 37:5–6 ESV

SEPTEMBER 2024

SUNDAY	MONDAY	TUESDAY	WEDNESDAY
1	2	3	4
	Labor Day		
8	9	10	11
15	16	17	18
22	23	24	25
First Day of Autumn			
29	30	1	2

THURSDAY	FRIDAY	SATURDAY
5	6	7
12	13	14
19	20	21
26	27	28
3	4	5

IN THE CLEFTS OF THE ROCK

Oh Lord! You hide me away in the cleft of the rock, in a place where I am safe from the goings-on around me. I'm Your dove, Your bride, and I'm waiting for You there, safely tucked away, and all in preparation for our time together.

I will meet You there today, Lord. I will hide myself from the cares of life long enough to spend holy time with You. There we will listen to one another. Truly listen. I will share my thoughts. You will share Your heart for me. We will grow and deepen our relationship, our love becoming more refined the longer we spend together.

Thank You for giving me a safe place to meet with You, Father! Thank You for reminding me that even with the chaos swirling around me, You yearn for me to pause long enough to spend holy moments with You.

Amen.

GOALS for this MONTH

- [ ] ....
- [ ] ....
- [ ] ....
- [ ] ....
- [ ] ....
- [ ] ....
- [ ] ....
- [ ] ....
- [ ] ....
- [ ] ....
- [ ] ....
- [ ] ....
- [ ] ....
- [ ] ....

My dove in the clefts of the rock, in the hiding places on the mountainside, show me your face, let me hear your voice; for your voice is sweet, and your face is lovely.
SONG OF SONGS 2:14 NIV

Father, Your Word tells me to guard my
heart and my mind, so that's what I will do.
May every day be a guarded day—guarded
by the peace that comes only from You.

SUNDAY, September 1

MONDAY, September 2   *Labor Day*

TUESDAY, September 3

WEDNESDAY, September 4

THURSDAY, September 5

FRIDAY, September 6

SATURDAY, September 7

The peace of God, which surpasses all understanding, will guard your hearts and your minds in Christ Jesus.
PHILIPPIANS 4:7 ESV

I will trust You, God, even when the path ahead looks slippery. With one word, You can keep me walking firm instead of taking an unnecessary tumble. Thanks for staying awake and watching over me, Lord!

SUNDAY, September 8

MONDAY, September 9

TUESDAY, September 10

WEDNESDAY, September 11

THURSDAY, September 12

FRIDAY, September 13

SATURDAY, September 14

He will not let your foot slip—he who watches over
you will not slumber; indeed, he who watches
over Israel will neither slumber nor sleep.
PSALM 121:3–4 NIV

Lord, Your Word says that if I'm faithful in the little things, You will give me bigger things. Are You waiting on me to prove that I can be faithful with what You've already given me, Lord? Guide me to the areas of my life that need tweaking, I pray.

SUNDAY, September 15

MONDAY, September 16

TUESDAY, September 17

WEDNESDAY, September 18

THURSDAY, September 19

FRIDAY, September 20

SATURDAY, September 21

"One who is faithful in a very little is also faithful in much, and one who is dishonest in a very little is also dishonest in much. If then you have not been faithful in the unrighteous wealth, who will entrust to you the true riches?"
LUKE 16:10–11 ESV

It's in Your great name, Lord, that I take refuge
and find salvation. It's in Your great name
that I overcome my struggles. And it's in Your
great name, Jesus, that I have victory and can
overcome no matter what I'm walking through.

SUNDAY, September 22   *First Day of Autumn*

....

....

....

....

MONDAY, September 23

....

....

....

....

TUESDAY, September 24

....

....

....

....

WEDNESDAY, September 25

....

....

....

....

THURSDAY, September 26

....

....

....

....

FRIDAY, September 27

....

....

....

....

SATURDAY, September 28

....

....

....

....

Some trust in chariots and some in horses,
but we trust in the name of the Lord our God.
PSALM 20:7 ESV

OCTOBER 2024

SUNDAY	MONDAY	TUESDAY	WEDNESDAY
29	30	1	2
6	7	8	9
13	14 *Columbus Day*	15	16
20	21	22	23
27	28	29	30

THURSDAY	FRIDAY	SATURDAY
3	4	5
10	11	12
17	18	19
24	25	26
31 *Halloween*	1	2

SEPTEMBER

S	M	T	W	T	F	S
1	2	3	4	5	6	7
8	9	10	11	12	13	14
15	16	17	18	19	20	21
22	23	24	25	26	27	28
29	30					

NOVEMBER

S	M	T	W	T	F	S
					1	2
3	4	5	6	7	8	9
10	11	12	13	14	15	16
17	18	19	20	21	22	23
24	25	26	27	28	29	30

TRUTH!

There's a lot of confusion in this world, Lord. It's hard to know what we can believe. Can we put our trust in the media? Can we put our trust in politicians? Can we put our trust in friends or family members? I don't think so! They let us down time and time again!

Truly, Lord, the only one who has fully earned my trust is You! I won't ever have to wonder when I turn to Your Word if what I'm reading is truth. It never changes. It's as real and as perfect today as it was thousands of years ago.

My heart will be at peace as I place my trust in You alone. I have none in heaven besides You. There's nothing I desire besides You!

What a trustworthy God You are!

Amen.

GOALS for this MONTH

- [ ] ....
- [ ] ....
- [ ] ....
- [ ] ....
- [ ] ....
- [ ] ....
- [ ] ....
- [ ] ....
- [ ] ....
- [ ] ....
- [ ] ....
- [ ] ....
- [ ] ....
- [ ] ....

*Whom have I in heaven but you? And earth
has nothing I desire besides you. My flesh and
my heart may fail, but God is the strength
of my heart and my portion forever.*

PSALM 73:25–26 NIV

I'm intrigued by this idea that Your peace surpasses all understanding, so I'm heading in Your direction, Lord, ready to do things Your way. Thank You for the reminder that I can live above these circumstances in front of me.

SUNDAY, September 29

....

....

....

....

MONDAY, September 30

....

....

....

....

TUESDAY, October 1

....

....

....

....

WEDNESDAY, October 2

THURSDAY, October 3

FRIDAY, October 4

SATURDAY, October 5

Do not be anxious about anything, but in everything
by prayer and supplication with thanksgiving
let your requests be made known to God.
And the peace of God, which surpasses
all understanding, will guard your
hearts and your minds in Christ Jesus.
PHILIPPIANS 4:6–7 ESV

I'm humbled by the cross, Lord. I'm broken by the cross. I'm healed by the cross. And I can never express my gratitude enough, but I will do my best to try to thank You for all that took place that awful, wonderful day. How grateful I am!

SUNDAY, October 6

....

....

....

....

MONDAY, October 7

....

....

....

....

TUESDAY, October 8

....

....

....

....

WEDNESDAY, October 9

THURSDAY, October 10

FRIDAY, October 11

SATURDAY, October 12

He himself bore our sins in his body on the tree,
that we might die to sin and live to
righteousness. By his wounds
you have been healed.
1 PETER 2:24 ESV

Of all the things You have ever spoken into existence, God, perhaps the most mesmerizing of all is the work You've done in my heart. It's more colorful than any rainbow, more active than any volcano, and more riveting than any mountain peak.

SUNDAY, October 13

....

....

....

....

MONDAY, October 14   *Columbus Day*

....

....

....

TUESDAY, October 15

....

....

....

....

WEDNESDAY, October 16

THURSDAY, October 17

FRIDAY, October 18

SATURDAY, October 19

Create in me a pure heart, O God,
and renew a steadfast spirit within me.
PSALM 51:10 NIV

Seeing You working in the lives of those I
love brings me great joy, Lord. We will grow
together in the knowledge of You, getting wiser
by the day as we learn Your great precepts.

SUNDAY, October 20

MONDAY, October 21

TUESDAY, October 22

WEDNESDAY, October 23

THURSDAY, October 24

FRIDAY, October 25

SATURDAY, October 26

My message and my preaching were not with
wise and persuasive words, but with a
demonstration of the Spirit's power,
so that your faith might not rest on
human wisdom, but on God's power.
1 Corinthians 2:4–5 niv

NOVEMBER 2024

SUNDAY	MONDAY	TUESDAY	WEDNESDAY
27	28	29	30
3 *Daylight Saving Time Ends*	4	5 *Election Day*	6
10	11 *Veterans Day*	12	13
17	18	19	20
24	25	26	27

THURSDAY	FRIDAY	SATURDAY
31	1	2
7	8	9
14	15	16
21	22	23
28	29	30
Thanksgiving Day		

OCTOBER

S	M	T	W	T	F	S
		1	2	3	4	5
6	7	8	9	10	11	12
13	14	15	16	17	18	19
20	21	22	23	24	25	26
27	28	29	30	31		

DECEMBER

S	M	T	W	T	F	S
1	2	3	4	5	6	7
8	9	10	11	12	13	14
15	16	17	18	19	20	21
22	23	24	25	26	27	28
29	30	31				

SONG OF PRAISE

I will praise You, Lord. Even when I don't feel like it. Even when things are not going my way. Even when my heart is overwhelmed. I will sing a song of praise to You because You are worthy, no matter what I am facing.

Your Word says that I should praise You ahead of the victory. There's great peace to be found in praise, so today I lift my hands and my heart. I lift my voice in adoration to You, not for what You are going to do for me—though I know You are a God of abundant blessings—but simply because of who You are.

My heart is quickened within me, Lord. May it exult in You all the days of my life!

Amen.

GOALS for this MONTH

- [ ] ....
- [ ] ....
- [ ] ....
- [ ] ....
- [ ] ....
- [ ] ....
- [ ] ....
- [ ] ....
- [ ] ....
- [ ] ....
- [ ] ....
- [ ] ....
- [ ] ....
- [ ] ....

*The LORD is my strength and my shield; in him
my heart trusts, and I am helped; my heart
exults, and with my song I give thanks to him.*
PSALM 28:7 ESV

Your plans for my life, Father? They were carefully thought out, long before I ever existed. You put far more care into preparing for my journey than I could ever do for any of my little excursions. Thanks for getting all the little details ironed out, Lord.

SUNDAY, October 27

....
....
....
....

MONDAY, October 28

....
....
....

TUESDAY, October 29

....
....
....
....

WEDNESDAY, October 30

....
....
....
....

THURSDAY, October 31   *Halloween*

....
....
....
....

FRIDAY, November 1

....
....
....
....

SATURDAY, November 2

....
....
....
....

*O Lord, you are my God; I will exalt you; I will
praise your name, for you have done wonderful
things, plans formed of old, faithful and sure.*
Isaiah 25:1 esv

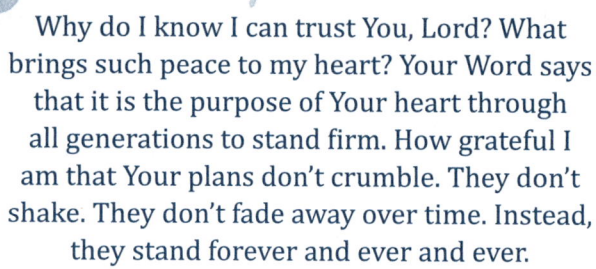

Why do I know I can trust You, Lord? What brings such peace to my heart? Your Word says that it is the purpose of Your heart through all generations to stand firm. How grateful I am that Your plans don't crumble. They don't shake. They don't fade away over time. Instead, they stand forever and ever and ever.

SUNDAY, November 3   *Daylight Saving Time Ends*

....

....

....

....

MONDAY, November 4

....

....

....

....

TUESDAY, November 5   *Election Day*

....

....

....

....

WEDNESDAY, November 6

THURSDAY, November 7

FRIDAY, November 8

SATURDAY, November 9

The plans of the LORD stand firm forever, the
purposes of his heart through all generations.
PSALM 33:11 NIV

I know I can trust You, Father. You've given me no reason not to! In fact, You've proven so many times over that You have my best interests at heart. Oh, how I appreciate Your love and care!

SUNDAY, November 10

....

....

....

....

MONDAY, November 11   *Veterans Day*

....

....

....

....

TUESDAY, November 12

....

....

....

....

WEDNESDAY, November 13

THURSDAY, November 14

FRIDAY, November 15

SATURDAY, November 16

Let the morning bring me word of your unfailing love, for I have put my trust in you. Show me the way I should go, for to you I entrust my life.
Psalm 143:8 niv

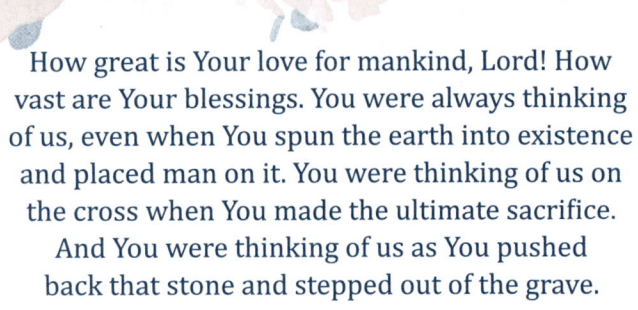

How great is Your love for mankind, Lord! How vast are Your blessings. You were always thinking of us, even when You spun the earth into existence and placed man on it. You were thinking of us on the cross when You made the ultimate sacrifice. And You were thinking of us as You pushed back that stone and stepped out of the grave.

SUNDAY, November 17

MONDAY, November 18

TUESDAY, November 19

WEDNESDAY, November 20

....
....
....
....

THURSDAY, November 21

....
....
....
....

FRIDAY, November 22

....
....
....
....

SATURDAY, November 23

....
....
....
....

How precious to me are your thoughts,
God! How vast is the sum of them!
PSALM 139:17 NIV

Heavenly Father, You are my refuge when trouble comes. That's all I need to remember when I'm starting to panic. You're close to me when I place my trust in You, never more than a prayer away. Thank You for being my stronghold in the day of trouble, Lord!

SUNDAY, November 24

MONDAY, November 25

TUESDAY, November 26

WEDNESDAY, November 27

....
....
....
....

THURSDAY, November 28   *Thanksgiving Day*

....
....
....
....

FRIDAY, November 29

....
....
....
....

SATURDAY, November 30

....
....
....
....

The LORD is good, a strong refuge when trouble comes. He is close to those who trust in him.
NAHUM 1:7 NLT

DECEMBER 2024

SUNDAY	MONDAY	TUESDAY	WEDNESDAY
1	2	3	4
8	9	10	11
15	16	17	18
22	23	24 *Christmas Eve*	25 *Christmas Day* *Hanukkah Begins at Sundown*
29	30	31 *New Year's Eve*	1

THURSDAY	FRIDAY	SATURDAY
5	6	7
12	13	14
19	20	21 *First Day of Winter*
26	27	28
2	3	4

NOVEMBER

S	M	T	W	T	F	S
					1	2
3	4	5	6	7	8	9
10	11	12	13	14	15	16
17	18	19	20	21	22	23
24	25	26	27	28	29	30

JANUARY

S	M	T	W	T	F	S
			1	2	3	4
5	6	7	8	9	10	11
12	13	14	15	16	17	18
19	20	21	22	23	24	25
26	27	28	29	30	31	

NOTHING I'VE DONE

I've been known to brag on myself a time or two, Lord. I perform some feat and feel pretty good about myself. I start to think I'm all that and a bag of chips. After giving myself a few pats on the back, I share what I've done with others, doing my best to sound humble as I brag about my accomplishment.

Maybe I will accomplish some good things in my lifetime, Lord. But Your Word tells me that nothing I'll ever do will come close to the free gift of salvation that You gave me. Every act, every feat, pales in comparison.

Salvation is such a glorious gift, and You gave it at such a high cost! Eternal life came not at my own hands, but at the hands of a Savior who allowed Himself to be crucified for my sins.

How grateful I am for the peace You bring through Your work on the cross, Lord. You, and only You, deserve praise!

Amen.

GOALS for this MONTH

- [ ] ....
- [ ] ....
- [ ] ....
- [ ] ....
- [ ] ....
- [ ] ....
- [ ] ....
- [ ] ....
- [ ] ....
- [ ] ....
- [ ] ....
- [ ] ....
- [ ] ....
- [ ] ....

*It is by grace you have been saved,
through faith—and this is not from
yourselves, it is the gift of God—not by
works, so that no one can boast.*
EPHESIANS 2:8–9 NIV

I want to be a blessing to everyone I come in contact with—not so that people will see me as holy, but because I love them, Lord. Give me Your passion and Your compassion for others, I pray. I want to be more like You.

SUNDAY, December 1

MONDAY, December 2

TUESDAY, December 3

WEDNESDAY, December 4

THURSDAY, December 5

FRIDAY, December 6

SATURDAY, December 7

*"And you know that God anointed Jesus of
Nazareth with the Holy Spirit and with power.
Then Jesus went around doing good and
healing all who were oppressed by
the devil, for God was with him."*
ACTS 10:38 NLT

May I be as forgiving and gracious to others as You have been to me, Father. If You can choose not to remember, maybe I can too. What peace I have knowing that You're not holding my sins against me.

SUNDAY, December 8

MONDAY, December 9

TUESDAY, December 10

WEDNESDAY, December 11

THURSDAY, December 12

FRIDAY, December 13

SATURDAY, December 14

Do not remember the rebellious sins of my youth. Remember me in the light of your unfailing love, for you are merciful, O Lord.
PSALM 25:7 NLT

Lord, You are and always have been the one to make sure I have everything I need, and for that I am so grateful. If You take care of the birds, giving them seed to eat, then I know You have me covered. So I will remain confident that I will see Your goodness, Lord. You've proven it time and time again, after all.

SUNDAY, December 15

MONDAY, December 16

TUESDAY, December 17

WEDNESDAY, December 18

THURSDAY, December 19

FRIDAY, December 20

SATURDAY, December 21   *First Day of Winter*

*I remain confident of this: I will see the goodness
of the Lord in the land of the living.*
Psalm 27:13 niv

One thing I'm learning about You, Lord—You don't go against Your nature. Ever. You simply can't. You won't deny Yourself in that way. Even if I am faithless, God, You are still faithful because it is always in Your nature to be so. Even when I'm unloving, You never are. You couldn't be.

SUNDAY, December 22

....

....

....

....

MONDAY, December 23

....

....

....

....

TUESDAY, December 24   *Christmas Eve*

....

....

....

....

WEDNESDAY, December 25

Christmas Day,
Hanukkah Begins at Sundown

THURSDAY, December 26

FRIDAY, December 27

SATURDAY, December 28

If we are faithless, he remains faithful—
for he cannot deny himself.
2 TIMOTHY 2:13 ESV

I take my delight in You, Your Word, and Your ways, Lord. When I live this way, I'm like a sturdy tree planted by streams of clear, cool water. I'll always be fruitful. I will have peace and abundant joy in my life. Everything I touch will prosper when I remain true to You, the one true God!

SUNDAY, December 29

....
....
....
....

MONDAY, December 30

....
....
....
....

TUESDAY, December 31   *New Year's Eve*

....
....
....
....

WEDNESDAY, January 1   *New Year's Day*

....

....

....

....

THURSDAY, January 2

....

....

....

....

FRIDAY, January 3

....

....

....

....

SATURDAY, January 4

....

....

....

....

Blessed is the one who does not walk in step with the wicked or stand in the way that sinners take or sit in the company of mockers, but whose delight is in the law of the LORD, and who meditates on his law day and night. That person is like a tree planted by streams of water, which yields its fruit in season and whose leaf does not wither—whatever they do prospers.

PSALM 1:1–3 NIV

CONTACTS

Name:

Address:

Phone:

Email:

Name:

Address:

Phone:

Email:

Name:

Address:

Phone:

Email:

Name:

Address:

Phone:

Email:

Name:

Address:

Phone:

Email:

CONTACTS

Name:

Address:

Phone:

Email:

Name:

Address:

Phone:

Email:

Name:

Address:

Phone:

Email:

Name:

Address:

Phone:

Email:

Name:

Address:

Phone:

Email:

CONTACTS

Name:

Address:

Phone:

Email:

Name:

Address:

Phone:

Email:

Name:

Address:

Phone:

Email:

Name:

Address:

Phone:

Email:

Name:

Address:

Phone:

Email:

CONTACTS

Name:

Address:

Phone:

Email:

Name:

Address:

Phone:

Email:

Name:

Address:

Phone:

Email:

Name:

Address:

Phone:

Email:

Name:

Address:

Phone:

Email:

CONTACTS

Name:

Address:

Phone:

Email:

Name:

Address:

Phone:

Email:

Name:

Address:

Phone:

Email:

Name:

Address:

Phone:

Email:

Name:

Address:

Phone:

Email:

CONTACTS

Name:

Address:

Phone:

Email:

Name:

Address:

Phone:

Email:

Name:

Address:

Phone:

Email:

Name:

Address:

Phone:

Email:

Name:

Address:

Phone:

Email:

CONTACTS

Name:

Address:

Phone:

Email:

Name:

Address:

Phone:

Email:

Name:

Address:

Phone:

Email:

Name:

Address:

Phone:

Email:

Name:

Address:

Phone:

Email:

CONTACTS

Name:

Address:

Phone:

Email:

Name:

Address:

Phone:

Email:

Name:

Address:

Phone:

Email:

Name:

Address:

Phone:

Email:

Name:

Address:

Phone:

Email:

CONTACTS

Name:

Address:

Phone:

Email:

Name:

Address:

Phone:

Email:

Name:

Address:

Phone:

Email:

Name:

Address:

Phone:

Email:

Name:

Address:

Phone:

Email:

CONTACTS

Name:

Address:

Phone:

Email:

Name:

Address:

Phone:

Email:

Name:

Address:

Phone:

Email:

Name:

Address:

Phone:

Email:

Name:

Address:

Phone:

Email:

CONTACTS

Name:

Address:

Phone:

Email:

Name:

Address:

Phone:

Email:

Name:

Address:

Phone:

Email:

Name:

Address:

Phone:

Email:

Name:

Address:

Phone:

Email:

CONTACTS

Name:

Address:

Phone:

Email:

Name:

Address:

Phone:

Email:

Name:

Address:

Phone:

Email:

Name:

Address:

Phone:

Email:

Name:

Address:

Phone:

Email:

CONTACTS

Name:

Address:

Phone:

Email:

Name:

Address:

Phone:

Email:

Name:

Address:

Phone:

Email:

Name:

Address:

Phone:

Email:

Name:

Address:

Phone:

Email:

CONTACTS

Name:

Address:

Phone:

Email:

Name:

Address:

Phone:

Email:

Name:

Address:

Phone:

Email:

Name:

Address:

Phone:

Email:

Name:

Address:

Phone:

Email:

2025

JANUARY
S M T W T F S
1 2 3 4
5 6 7 8 9 10 11
12 13 14 15 16 17 18
19 20 21 22 23 24 25
26 27 28 29 30 31

FEBRUARY
S M T W T F S
1
2 3 4 5 6 7 8
9 10 11 12 13 14 15
16 17 18 19 20 21 22
23 24 25 26 27 28

MARCH
S M T W T F S
1
2 3 4 5 6 7 8
9 10 11 12 13 14 15
16 17 18 19 20 21 22
23 24 25 26 27 28 29
30 31

APRIL
S M T W T F S
1 2 3 4 5
6 7 8 9 10 11 12
13 14 15 16 17 18 19
20 21 22 23 24 25 26
27 28 29 30

MAY
S M T W T F S
1 2 3
4 5 6 7 8 9 10
11 12 13 14 15 16 17
18 19 20 21 22 23 24
25 26 27 28 29 30 31

JUNE
S M T W T F S
1 2 3 4 5 6 7
8 9 10 11 12 13 14
15 16 17 18 19 20 21
22 23 24 25 26 27 28
29 30

JULY
S M T W T F S
1 2 3 4 5
6 7 8 9 10 11 12
13 14 15 16 17 18 19
20 21 22 23 24 25 26
27 28 29 30 31

AUGUST
S M T W T F S
1 2
3 4 5 6 7 8 9
10 11 12 13 14 15 16
17 18 19 20 21 22 23
24 25 26 27 28 29 30
31

SEPTEMBER
S M T W T F S
1 2 3 4 5 6
7 8 9 10 11 12 13
14 15 16 17 18 19 20
21 22 23 24 25 26 27
28 29 30

OCTOBER
S M T W T F S
1 2 3 4
5 6 7 8 9 10 11
12 13 14 15 16 17 18
19 20 21 22 23 24 25
26 27 28 29 30 31

NOVEMBER
S M T W T F S
1
2 3 4 5 6 7 8
9 10 11 12 13 14 15
16 17 18 19 20 21 22
23 24 25 26 27 28 29
30

DECEMBER
S M T W T F S
1 2 3 4 5 6
7 8 9 10 11 12 13
14 15 16 17 18 19 20
21 22 23 24 25 26 27
28 29 30 31

2026

JANUARY
S M T W T F S
1 2 3
4 5 6 7 8 9 10
11 12 13 14 15 16 17
18 19 20 21 22 23 24
25 26 27 28 29 30 31

FEBRUARY
S M T W T F S
1 2 3 4 5 6 7
8 9 10 11 12 13 14
15 16 17 18 19 20 21
22 23 24 25 26 27 28

MARCH
S M T W T F S
1 2 3 4 5 6 7
8 9 10 11 12 13 14
15 16 17 18 19 20 21
22 23 24 25 26 27 28
29 30 31

APRIL
S M T W T F S
1 2 3 4
5 6 7 8 9 10 11
12 13 14 15 16 17 18
19 20 21 22 23 24 25
26 27 28 29 30

MAY
S M T W T F S
1 2
3 4 5 6 7 8 9
10 11 12 13 14 15 16
17 18 19 20 21 22 23
24 25 26 27 28 29 30
31

JUNE
S M T W T F S
1 2 3 4 5 6
7 8 9 10 11 12 13
14 15 16 17 18 19 20
21 22 23 24 25 26 27
28 29 30

JULY
S M T W T F S
1 2 3 4
5 6 7 8 9 10 11
12 13 14 15 16 17 18
19 20 21 22 23 24 25
26 27 28 29 30 31

AUGUST
S M T W T F S
1
2 3 4 5 6 7 8
9 10 11 12 13 14 15
16 17 18 19 20 21 22
23 24 25 26 27 28 29
30 31

SEPTEMBER
S M T W T F S
1 2 3 4 5
6 7 8 9 10 11 12
13 14 15 16 17 18 19
20 21 22 23 24 25 26
27 28 29 30

OCTOBER
S M T W T F S
1 2 3
4 5 6 7 8 9 10
11 12 13 14 15 16 17
18 19 20 21 22 23 24
25 26 27 28 29 30 31

NOVEMBER
S M T W T F S
1 2 3 4 5 6 7
8 9 10 11 12 13 14
15 16 17 18 19 20 21
22 23 24 25 26 27 28
29 30

DECEMBER
S M T W T F S
1 2 3 4 5
6 7 8 9 10 11 12
13 14 15 16 17 18 19
20 21 22 23 24 25 26
27 28 29 30 31